Vulnerability

&

Dreams

Jay Caniel

ISBN: **0692077464**
ISBN-13: **978-0692077467**

DEDICATION

To all the dreamers in this life.
To the universe up high.
To the territory that spreads wide.
To the unlimited capacity of happiness inside.
To smiles that make smiles.
To auras that make it pleasant to be alive.
To the visionaries who never lost sight.
To the strong,
The bold,
The ones who go the extra mile.
To the great intentions and all the people who subscribe.
To One Race and those of us against divide…

Thank you, from Little Brown Eyes.

ACKNOWLEDGMENTS

I just want to thank Ma (Geneva Maynard) and my brother Lesroy for all of the inspiration and support they have given me through my life. I love you.

Jay Caniel

VULNERABILITY

CONFESSION

Confession…
Never thought I could write.
I just figured they were weird thoughts in my mind.
In the dark I would hide…
Little insecure brown eyes…
At night I would dream about flying.
During the day I was a lion…
Traveling to a world beyond my mind.
A happy place, I surmise…
It's hard with the normalcy of ideals in this life.
To be great…
To be bold…
To never fold…
To hold on to the instincts deep in your soul.
To be a butterfly when a caterpillar is only thing spoke…
I beat the odds and I know…

EVERY MONTH, EVERY YEAR

Every month… every year…
Every minute draws me nearer…
Picturing the end. How do I fare?
Every flight…every risk…
Every mountain climbed or missed…
Striving to learn more of who we are…
It's hard.
Leaving the past that didn't serve us behind.
Just not wanting to effect the mind.
Being vulnerable enough to smile when we're broken inside.
Just need someone to confide in…
Where are the real people?
Where do I find them?

PAIN

I couldn't live without the pain.
The picture I painted filled with stains.
Blood, sweat, and tears encased my name.
Maybe I had a plan.
Pure intentions where I stand.
Wanted to see the people thriving, man.
Took off never knowing how I would land.
But never seemed concerned 'cause if I remained I knew I could
Never be…
I would never see…
Like I would be concealed and never free.

DARKNESS

Darkness…
I remember first meeting light…
That feeling inside…
Like being betrayed…
A cringe in the stomach…
Like walking in a straight line.
Living in confines…
Confused and frustrated beyond life…

Darkness…
I remember first meeting light…
Opening eyes for the first time.
Unfamiliar with my insides.

OFTEN BADGERED BY SUCCESS

Often badgered by success…
It took being a man to digest…
Force-fed…
Lead to believe…
Lost in the illusion of someone else's dreams…
Till one day I questioned the machine…
What really separates us as human beings?
Is all they emphasize what it's cracked up to be?
What am I making if I got to fake it to be?

I BROKE IN

I broke in…
Fighting for life…
Fighting for an endless reservoir of some type.
Is it money?
Happiness?
Love?
Or do I want societal likes?
On the road but not sure what fulfills me tonight.
Young and unwise…
Growing, but no one to raise this young lion.
Got three eyes but still blind…
No feel for what's real…
Drowning as I walk down these streets.
How do I heal?
Am I willing to go through pain to be real?
Go left when they go right?
Do I want to grow on the inside?
Maybe be a legend of my own life?

RUNNING

Running…
But holding on to fear…
Staring at a star
Dazed…
In the mirror my vulnerable face…
I don't like the taste.
So my mind makes haste
Toward a new start…
A new day…
Thinking back to when I was a kid.
The voices, what did they say?
How we played fearless all day!
Ignoring the bells…
Never believed in spells…
Our smiles gave way…
Like a breath of fresh air…
Happiness, love and freedom paint away.

THAT MOMENT

Covering my eyes…
Like I don't want to wake up…
Tell me this is my life.
Taking deep breaths…
Checking my pulse.
Long looks in the mirror…
Lesroy's smile…
That moment when
Real life becomes better that the dream.
Impossible suddenly within reach.
That moment when
The voice inside is no longer concealed…
And it starts to teach.
That moment when we start to reach…
That moment when
We become one…
Whole.
Loved.
Vulnerable enough to heal…
That moment when
Insecurities flee…

In these moments, we become free.

Jay Caniel

THE BUTTERFLIES FLOAT AROUND IN MY HEAD

The butterflies float around in my head...
The shame of the caterpillar is now dead...
But the trails remind us of where we've been.
The memories of the voices of doubt became deaf.
We gave them no good soil in which to grow.
Kept the good shit in our hearts for sure.
The dark played a part...
In the silence we gain an understanding of who we are...
Spent nights fighting against ourselves.
This must be the craziness they eluded to in the beginning.
But in the end the box says genius instead.
Most of us right from the start.
Hold on to your thoughts.
We can change the world with one spark.

al

BEAUTIFUL BUT WILD

Beautiful but wild…
A sight for sore eyes…
Like your color represents the spectrum of life…
Alone in a field you reside.
Or maybe just in my mind…
Rare but common to keen eyes.
Your presence creates a sigh…
Some things are unexplainable in life.
Bloom.
I hope you bloom more life.
Teaching us to be bold and one of a kind.
Teaching us that our imperfections create beauty and light…
Like perfect never existed.
Vulnerability got us lifted…
Wildflower, you inspire our lives.

Jay Caniel

I LOST THE WORLD

I lost the world.
Dreaming within.
Being bold and fearless.
I lost the world…
Jumping off cliffs…
Skipping to my own beat.
Thinking happiness was sweet.
I lost the world.
Swimming in the thoughts in my head.
Going higher when low was in.
I lost the world…
Maybe it was the color of my skin.
Or the light that I carried within.
I lost the world…
Being myself.
I lost the world, but I found a gem…

EXPECTATIONS

The sun rises like the expectations in my mind.
Set the pace for great intentions in life.
Be bold going after doubt, insecurities, and fears.
Running away is like joining the mediocrity of society.

Remember…
Strong is beautiful…
Kind is cool…
Knowing yourself is the best school.
And the world worships the original.
I'm talking about you.

WHAT IF?

What if my eyes never drifted?
Like Third Eye intuition was dead…
What if my insecurities never bled?
Walking around covering up with a band-aide instead…
What if the voices inside never lead?
Silenced by society, I guess.
What if my heart beat at the frequencies it saw
And not what it sees?
I'm wondering who would I be?
Stagnant like unmoving water…
Never emptying or replenishing naturally…
One day I broke free.
Determined to be.
'Cause I knew someone captive was watching me…
Now we're all free.

DREAMS

THE LITTLE BOY WHO DREAMS

The little boy who dreams
Wears his heart on his sleeve
Creating a life from a seed...
Watching it grow in a creek...
The journey mapped on the canvas of his mind.
The possibilities of greatness produces a smile...
Light...
So he skips for a while...
Painting happiness for all of humanity's eyes.
Painting wealth through good character, kindness, love and compassion
For all mankind.

The little girl who dreams
Ventured out beyond the trees...
Experiencing life beyond belief...
Discovering we can be anything we want to be.
Her smile means kind...
Compassion in her eyes.
Protecting the pride...
Birthing a legacy worthwhile.

LIKE CLAY WE TAKE SHAPE

Like clay, we take shape.
The inevitable we create…
Walking, talking, displaying our faith…
No streets so we paved our own ways…
No superheroes so we saved our own days.

I WANT TO FLY

I want to fly…
Feeling the wind on my face as I soar through the skies
Like a kite I want to glide…
Playing in the clouds as my imagination runs wild.
I want to smile…
Feeling the happiness flow from inside.
To the dimple on my face…
To the crinkles around my eyes.
I want to see humanity as one in this life.
One Race.

REFLECTIONS

No pot to piss in…
But a mind that's living.
I took the ideas of my heart
The air in my lungs
The strength from my feet…
Even mustered up the courage to see…
Begging my hands to please stay with me…
Told my mind "One day we will be free…"
During frustrated nights I drew a window for breeze…
In the mirror I see
Poverty
In the mirror I see
Opportunity.
I looked and I looked…
I looked until I saw myself free.
The perfect image to aspire to be.
In the mirror I see humanity.
I see our dreams.
Our hopes.
I see the harvest of the seed…
I see how time heals.
I saw a frown turn to a smile.
I saw a pauper turn into a King before sunrise.
I saw the rain turn to sunshine.
I see the beauty that's within you and me.

Jay Caniel

DEAR DREAMERS

Dear Dreamers,
What happens when it becomes real?
You become a target...
Paying for their insecurities.
Like you never earned your keep.
Like it was all given to you...
Like you didn't work while they were sleep.
Jumped off the cliff and swam to Free.
They tell you to be all you can be.
And when you do,
They call you crazy.

But Dreamer,
You survived the cliff!
Almost drowned but you continued to breathe.
All the nights you worked while the world preferred to sleep...
All the times you believed...
Alone listening to the silence speak.
There is nothing like being free.

WILD AND FREE

Wild and free
With a song in my mind
And big smiles within me…
Happiness within reach
The world at my feet…
Skipping.
Thinking freely.
Painting the world that I see.
Striving to be the best human being.
Overcoming the fears that they teach…
Opening their eyes to see.
The stars are aligned within our bodies.

Wild and free…
With a song in my mind.
And big smiles within me.

IF I NEVER KNEW

If I never knew
If I never grew
If I never believed
Or seen the beauty a life could achieve.
If I cast away my hopes
And squandered my dreams.
If I allowed my soul to be soulless in the streets,
Then I wouldn't be me.

One day I broke free...
Accepted my faults
Looked into my brown eyes and believed.
Then the vision came to me.
We created everything we see.
Now I know!

I grow!
I believe!
I've seen the beauty a life could achieve.
I breathe into my hopes
And allow myself to dream.
Feeding my soul.
Creating legacy.
Now I am free!

THE FACES

The faces
The smiles
The reasons why
Wings appear at the thought of flight.
Things happen when you act in life.
Like my heart big enough to keep humanity alive.
Thinking I might be delusional
As I take the jump the first time.
Survived…
Thrived in every environment
Just to look you in your eyes
Breathe air into you…
Inspire.

TO MY DREAMS

To my dreams,
You're unreal.
How you persist with such fervor is beyond me.

YOU DON'T NEED BRIDGES

You don't need bridges when you can fly.

SO I HAD THIS DREAM

So I had this dream...
Where I could be the kid in me.
Travel the world and wake up on a random beach...
Like free.
Playing in my thoughts is so me...
Surrounded by foreigners
But when I smile we agree.
That crinkle around the eyes means happy.

LIKE A BIG LIGHT

Like a big light…
This time
Maybe we can let our minds go free…
Chasing the wind aimlessly.
Riding the wave of happy.
Swimming in a stream of love…
Like a big light.
We should stay kids for a while.
Smiling and giving the others no choice but to smile.
This time we'll let the world feel our heart beat.
Screaming "ONE RACE!" till the Universe accepts this idea.
Extending our hands to mankind.
This time we won't hide.
Refusing to let any of our dreams die.
Like a big light,
We'll shine.
Like eagles we'll glide

I'M HOLDING ON TO THE DREAMS

I'm holding on to the dreams.
Holding on to what's real.
Believing everything within me.
Even believed outrageous could be achieved.
Like I painted the faces before me.
In the back of my mind.
In the dark.
I lost sleep
But their laughter awakens me.

About the Author

Jay Caniel is a proud native of tropical St. Thomas, USVI who currently splits his time between homes in the U.S. and Europe. He developed a love for writing as a boy, writing in his journal almost daily for much of his life. It has become his most cherished form of expression. Jay hopes to inspire and empower others through his writings and philanthropic works.

www.ingramcontent.com/pod-product-compliance
Lightning Source LLC
Chambersburg PA
CBHW041811040426
42449CB00004B/148